Chocolate Delights

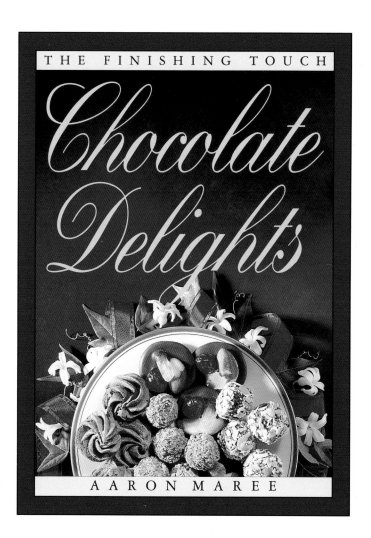

THE FINISHING TOUCH

Chocolate Delights

AARON MAREE

CASSELL

To my sister, Alison Larson
(who has been an avid chocolate lover
for as long as I can remember),
her husband John and my nephew Matthew.

CASSELL
Villiers House
41-47 Strand
London WC2N 5JE

First published in the UK by Cassell 1993 by arrangement with
CollinsAngus&Robertson Publishers Pty Ltd

First published in Australia in 1993 by
CollinsAngus&Robertson Publishers Pty Limited
25 Ryde Road, Pymble NSW 2073 Australia

British Library Cataloguing-in-Publication data:
A catalogue record for this book is available from the British Library

ISBN 0 304 34257 2

Photographer: Andre Martin
Stylist: Karen Carter
Assistant Stylist: Katie Mitchell

Printed in the People's Republic of China

Contents

Brandy Paste Truffles (above), Chocolate Coffee Truffles (below)

CHAPTER ONE

Petits Fours

Today, chocolate is at a peak of popularity. Any dessert
seems to be more appealing when filled, topped, drizzled
or dipped in chocolate. Petits fours are no exception.
These tiny dessert delights look and taste fantastic
when chocolate is a part of their design.

◆

Chocolate was first used by the Aztecs as currency in
its unprocessed form — the cacao bean. It was brought
to Europe by Columbus in 1494, however it wasn't
until the seventeeth century that knowledge of the use
of cacao beans spread through Europe and Chocolate
Houses were opened in London. Because of a spelling
error, cacao beans became known as cocoa beans in the
English speaking world. The rest, as they say,
is history.

Brandy Paste Truffles

◆

*175 g (6 oz) thickened (double
or heavy) cream
105 g (4 oz) unsalted butter
420 g (15 oz) dark (plain or
semi-sweet) chocolate, melted
75 ml (2 ½ fl oz) brandy
240 g (8 ½ oz) hot chocolate drinking
powder*

Place the cream and butter into a
saucepan and bring slowly to the boil.
Add the melted dark chocolate and
stir to a smooth liquid, free of any
lumps. Add the brandy and mix in
well. Pour the mixture into a mixing
bowl and place in the refrigerator.
Stir every few minutes until the
mixture becomes smooth and thick
enough to pipe. Fit a 1 ½ cm (½ in)
star-shaped piping nozzle on to a
piping (pastry) bag and fill with the
truffle mixture. Pipe star or rosette
shapes on to a baking parchment-
lined tray. When the tray is full,
place in the refrigerator and allow the
truffles to set hard. Remove from the
refrigerator and dust each truffle with
the chocolate drinking powder. Place
on to a serving dish and serve immediately or place in an airtight container
and store in the refrigerator until
required.

Makes 36

Chocolate Coffee Truffles

◆

240 g (8 ½ oz) thickened (double
or heavy) cream
90 g (3 oz) unsalted butter
3 tablespoons (½ oz) instant coffee
granules
600 g (21 oz) white chocolate,
chopped finely
360 g (12 ½ oz) white chocolate,
melted
1 ½ cups (8 ½ oz) icing (powdered)
sugar, sifted

Place the cream and butter into a saucepan and allow to come to the boil. Quickly whisk the coffee granules into the boiling mixture and when dissolved remove the saucepan from the heat and immediately add the chopped chocolate. Allow it to sit for several minutes. Then stir the mixture until it is smooth and free of any chocolate lumps. Pour the warm mixture into a bowl and cover with plastic (cling) wrap. Refrigerate for 12 hours.

Remove the mixture from the refrigerator and using a melon baller dipped in hot water, place balls of the mixture on to a tray lined with plastic (cling) wrap. Place the tray in the freezer for 20 minutes to allow the balls to firm.

Sift the icing sugar on to a baking tray. Melt the second amount of the white chocolate. Dip your fingers into the cooled melted chocolate and then roll each ball in your fingers to coat with chocolate. Quickly drop each ball into the sifted icing sugar. Shake the tray to ensure that each truffle is completely coated in icing sugar. After coating all the truffles place them on a serving platter if they are to be served immediately, or store them in an airtight container and refrigerate.

Makes 36

Milk Chocolate Truffles

240 g (8 ½ oz) thickened (double or heavy) cream
630 g (22 oz) milk chocolate, chopped finely
90 g (3 oz) unsalted butter, softened
300 g (10 ½ oz) milk chocolate, coarsely grated
360 g (12 ½ oz) milk chocolate, melted
icing (powdered) sugar, for dusting

Place the cream into a saucepan and allow it to come to the boil. Remove saucepan from the heat and add the finely chopped chocolate. Allow the mixture to stand for several minutes before stirring to a smooth paste, free of chocolate lumps. Add the butter immediately and stir slowly until it is completely incorporated into the chocolate mixture. Pour the mixture into a bowl and cover tightly with plastic (cling) wrap. Refrigerate until firm (12 hours or overnight). Remove the mixture from the refrigerator. Using a melon baller which has been dipped in warm water, place balls of the mixture on to a tray lined with plastic (cling) wrap. When all of the balls have been arranged on the tray, place in the freezer for 20 minutes to allow the balls to firm. Place the coarsely grated milk chocolate into a tray. Remove the tray of chilled balls from the refrigerator. Dip your fingers into the melted milk chocolate, then roll one ball at a time between your fingers to coat with chocolate before dropping it into the grated chocolate. Roll them around in the tray to cover completely. Place the truffles on a serving dish or in an airtight storage container, and refrigerate until required. Prior to serving dust lightly with icing sugar.

Makes 36

Milk Chocolate Truffles

Dark Chocolate Truffles

Dark Chocolate Truffles

250 g (9 oz) thickened (double
or heavy) cream
600 g (21 oz) dark (plain or
semi-sweet) chocolate, chopped
60 g (2 oz) unsalted butter, softened
300 g (12 ½ oz) dark (plain or
semi-sweet) chocolate, melted
1 ¾ cups (7 oz) flaked almonds,
lightly roasted

Place the cream into a saucepan and slowly bring to the boil. Add the chopped chocolate to the boiling mixture. Remove from the heat. Allow the chocolate to melt for several minutes before stirring to a smooth paste, free of any chocolate lumps. Add the butter and stir until completely incorporated. Pour the mixture into a bowl and cover with plastic (cling) wrap before refrigerating for 12 hours or overnight.

Remove the mixture from the refrigerator. Using a melon baller dipped frequently into warm water, place balls of the mixture on to a tray lined with plastic (cling) wrap. When all the mixture has been arranged on the tray, place in the freezer for 20 minutes to allow the balls to firm.

Place the flaked almonds on to a baking tray (sheet). Dip your fingers into the melted dark (plain or semi-sweet) chocolate and roll the truffles, one at a time, into the chocolate before dropping them into the flaked almonds. Roll the tray around to ensure the balls are completely covered. Allow the chocolate to set before removing the balls from the tray. Serve immediately or store in an airtight container and refrigerate until required. These truffles will keep for 1–2 weeks.

Makes 36

DISPLAYING TRUFFLES

The following simple ideas for displaying truffles add a special finishing touch to dinner parties or when entertaining.

Truffle Tree

Select 24 of your best truffles and carefully insert a toothpick or skewer into the base of each one. Place the skewers into an orange covered with a piece of material. Place them so that all the truffles touch.

This form of display is very quick and simple and the aroma of the orange mixed with the chocolate makes for a certain hit at the end of any meal.

Croquembouche de Truffe

Even simpler than the Truffle Tree is this pyramid or tower of truffles. Take an ice cream cone and dip it into dark (plain or semi-sweet), milk or white chocolate. Set the cone upright on a tray lined with baking parchment, with the pointy end upwards. Before the chocolate sets, begin pressing truffles on to the sides of the cone starting at the base. On top of the first layer place another layer and so on till you reach the top of the cone. Allow the pyramid to set firm before dusting with icing (powdered) sugar and serving.

Grape Vine

This truffle display looks sensational for buffets and is simple to construct. Arrange a group of truffles into a pile on a large plate to resemble a cluster of grapes. Using a small amount of melted chocolate, pipe a large 'T' for the branch on to a sheet of baking parchment and allow this to set firm in the refrigerator before placing at the top of the cluster. For greater effect make some chocolate leaves (see below for details) and pipe some curly lines of chocolate along the branch to resemble grape vine tendrils.

Note: To make chocolate leaves, spread a thin amount of dark (plain or semi-sweet) chocolate on to fresh clean green leaves. Allow the chocolate to set in the refrigerator before peeling away the leaves from the chocolate. The leaves need to be shiny in texture and well-veined. Should the leaves stick to the chocolate, lightly oil the leaves and then repeat the process.

Grape Vine (above), Croquembouche de Truffe (below)

Chocolate Cups

Chocolate Cups

◆

The paper cases used to produce
these are available in most
department store cookery
sections, in specialist chocolate
or confectionery shops and
homeware stores.

*300 g (10 ½ oz) dark (plain or
semi-sweet) chocolate, melted
50–60 paper petit four cups*

FILLING
*210 g (7 ½ oz) milk chocolate,
melted
500 ml (17 fl oz) thickened (double
or heavy) cream*

*extra dark (plain or semi-sweet)
chocolate, melted, for drizzling*

Separate the petit four cups into
stacked groups of two or three to
strengthen the case. Place all the
petit four cups on a tray.

Dip your finger into the melted
dark chocolate and coat the inside of
each case. When the chocolate has
set, once again coat the inside of each
cup with your finger dipped in chocolate. Make certain that the chocolate
is spread to the very rim of the paper
case without actually sitting on top or
spilling over the top of the case. This
would make removal very difficult.
When all the cases have been given a
second coating, allow them to set
firm while making the filling.

Very carefully peel off the paper
cases from each chocolate cup. If the
chocolate is softened by the heat of
your hands, place the tray of chocolate cups in the refrigerator for several
minutes. Fill each cup to the rim
with the creamed chocolate mixture.
When all cups have been filled, place
the tray into the refrigerator for 1
hour.

Place a small amount of melted
dark chocolate in a paper piping
(pastry) bag. Drizzle chocolate over
the top of each cup. Serve with
coffee. Alternatively you could float
a chocolate cup in your coffee and
allow it to melt as you drink.

FILLING
Melt the chocolate until it is smooth
and warm. Add the cream to the
chocolate and whisk very quickly so
that the chocolate does not set firm.
Once the cream and chocolate are
combined into a smooth paste stop
whisking. (If the chocolate sets hard
or the mixture looks split or curdled,
place it over a pot of simmering water
and stir until completely melted and
smooth.) Allow the filling mixture to
cool completely before spooning into
the chocolate cups. Add extra cream
to the mixture if it is not of pouring
consistency.

Makes 24

1. *Make the chocolate cup by dipping your finger into the melted chocolate and coating the inside of each case.*

3. *Fill each cup to the rim with the creamed chocolate mixture.*

2. *Make the filling by adding cream to the melted chocolate.*

4. *Decorate the chocolate cups by drizzling chocolate over the top.*

Rocher Chocolates

◆

2 cups (7 ½ oz) slivered almonds
¾ cup (4 oz) icing (powdered) sugar
30 ml (1 fl oz) Cointreau or
orange liqueur
210 g (7 ½ oz) milk chocolate, melted

Preheat oven to 180°C (350°F).

Place the almonds, icing sugar and Cointreau into a small bowl and stir until combined and the mixture is slightly moist.

Spread this mixture on to a baking tray (sheet) and place into the pre-heated oven. Remove the mixture every 3–4 minutes and turn with a palette knife so that it is evenly coloured and cooked.

After about 20 minutes the icing sugar should lose its powdery look and begin to crystallise around the almonds. Leave the almonds in the oven for a further 10 minutes to brown evenly. Remove the tray and turn the mixture occasionally, to allow the almonds to cool. Once cooled, break the mixture into bite-size pieces and place in a bowl. Pour in the melted chocolate and stir so it completely covers the almond mixture. Spoon small amounts of the mixture on to a baking tray lined with baking parchment. Allow the chocolates to set firm in the refrigerator before serving with coffee.

Note: If you keep these petits fours in an airtight container (in the refrigerator) they will last for weeks.

Makes 24

1. Spread the almond, icing sugar and Cointreau mixture into a baking tray.

2. Break the cool almond mixture into bite-size pieces.

3. Stir in the melted chocolate so it completely covers the almond mixture.

Rocher Chocolates

USING LEFTOVER CHOCOLATE

The only pitfall in making chocolates and truffles is that there is always leftover chocolate from breakages, drips and mistakes, usually with other ingredients in it. This scrap chocolate cannot be returned to your pot of good smooth chocolate.

Chocolate Fruit Bark

◆

There are several ways in which to use this leftover chocolate. One way is to remelt it and add extra nuts and fruits to it. The type and amount can be up to you. After adding these ingredients spread on to a sheet of baking parchment and press more fruit and nuts on top. Allow it to set hard in the refrigerator. Once set simply break into small bite-size pieces and serve.

Chocolate Tuiles

◆

A second way to use leftover chocolate is to melt it and spoon it on to small squares (5 x 5 cm (2 x 2 ½ in)) cut from a plastic bag. Use a spatula to spread the chocolate into round discs. Before the chocolate discs set, drape the plastic over a rolling pin or cylindrical object and allow to set.

Once firm remove from the cylindrical object, and carefully peel away the plastic square for further use. Lightly dust the Chocolate Tuiles with icing (powdered) sugar before arranging on a serving platter.

Chocolate Florentines

◆

Another way to use leftover chocolate is to melt it and spoon it on to baking parchment in small rounded mounds. Press small pieces of glacé (candied) pineapple, cherries and whole brazil nuts into the top of the chocolate mounds. Allow the mounds to set firm, then peel from the parchment and dust lightly with icing sugar.

Chocolate Fruit and Nut Truffles

◆

Add chopped fruit and nuts to the melted left over chocolate and use this to coat truffles. Once rolled in the chocolate nut mix the truffles could then be rolled in icing (powdered) sugar or cocoa as a decorative finish.

Deluxe Petits Fours

◆

You could also coat petits fours which need to be rolled or lightly coated in chocolate, in the fruit, nut and chocolate mixture. Both chocolate petits fours and truffles can be stored in airtight containers. These petits fours taste delicious combined with the fruit, nut and chocolate.

Quick Coconut Clusters

To a bowl of leftover melted chocolate, add enough toasted shredded coconut to stiffen the mixture until it is of a consistency that can be spooned on to baking parchment and will hold its shape.

Allow these shapes to set firm in the refrigerator and once they are hard, dip them into clean dark (plain or semi-sweet) chocolate, drizzle them with different coloured chocolate or you could even roll them in cocoa, icing (powdered) sugar or drinking chocolate before serving them with strong coffee.

Nut Clusters

Roast some finely chopped nuts of your choice on a baking tray. Roast them to a light golden brown, then allow to cool. Spoon small amounts of the leftover melted chocolate on to the cooled nuts and stir it in, flattening the mixture. Place small spoonfuls of the chocolate-covered nuts on to baking parchment and allow them to set firm. You can also add handfuls of dried fruit (such as finely cut apricots, currants or mixed (candied) peel) and fold this through the chocolate and nut mixture and then spoon on to the tray to set.

Chocolate Fingers

One of the simplest ways to use leftover melted chocolate is to add one or two drops of an oil-based flavouring (for example, mint or peppermint essence (extract)). Stir through the chocolate, then pour the mixture on to a baking parchment-lined tray and allow to set. Once set, cut into very fine fingers of 5 cm (2 in) long and 1 cm (⅓ in) wide. Serve these intensely flavoured chocolate delights with coffee for a wicked treat!

Chocolate Fruit Bark (above), Chocolate Tuiles (centre), Chocolate Florentines (below)

Chocolate Orange Sticks

3 large oranges of a good colour
1 ¼ cups (10 ½ oz) white
granulated sugar
250 ml (9 fl oz) water
200 g (7 oz) dark (plain or semi-sweet)
chocolate, melted
60 g (2 oz) unsalted butter, melted

Wash and clean the oranges. Using a sharp knife, cut long thin strips of rind from the oranges. Make sure the rind is free of white pith and flesh. Cut the rind into thinner strips. Place the orange strips into a saucepan of boiling water for 30 seconds. Remove and allow to drain. Place the water and sugar into another saucepan and bring slowly to the boil as the sugar dissolves. Place the orange strips in the sugar mixture and allow to boil for 8 minutes. (If the sugar mixture is beginning to brown slightly, add another 250 ml (8 ½ fl oz) of water and reboil.) Remove the orange strips and allow to sit on a wire cooling rack for approximately 12 hours or overnight.

Mix the chocolate and butter in a small bowl. Use a fork to dip each orange strip into the chocolate and allow the strips to sit on a sheet of baking parchment until the chocolate has set. If the chocolate will not set at room temperature, place the sheet of orange sticks on to a tray and refrigerate for 30 minutes.

Makes 15–18

Chocolate Orange Sticks

Christmas Logs

◆

*150 ml (5 fl oz) thickened (double
or heavy) cream
450 g (16 oz) milk chocolate, melted
600 g (21 oz) green-coloured marzipan
(see p. 62) or almond paste
300 g (10 ½ oz) dark (plain or
semi-sweet) chocolate, melted
icing (powdered) sugar, for dusting*

Make ganache by bringing the cream
to the boil in a saucepan. Remove
from the heat and immediately add
the milk chocolate. Stir until
smooth. Place the ganache in the
refrigerator and stir until it becomes
firm enough to pipe.

Roll out the marzipan in a square
shape (½ cm (¼ in) thick) on a lightly
floured bench (counter) top. Place the
ganache into a piping (pastry) bag,
fitted with a 1 cm (⅓ in) plain round
nozzle. Pipe lines of ganache on to
the marzipan 2 cm (¾ in) apart.
When you have finished piping, cut
the marzipan between each piped line.
Place in the refrigerator to harden for
5–10 minutes.

Pinch each strip of marzipan
around the chocolate ganache. Make
sure the join is closed up. Using a
pastry brush, brush the melted dark
chocolate over the outside of the
marzipan. Give each roll a good coating. Allow this to set before cutting
the log into 2–3 cm (¾–1 in) slices.

Dust lightly with icing sugar before
serving.

Makes 36

*1. Pipe lines of the ganache on to the marzipan,
2 cm (¾ in) apart.*

*2. Cut the marzipan down the centre between
each line of ganache.*

*3. Pinch each strip of marzipan around the
chocolate ganache.*

Christmas Logs

Kirsch Praline Delights

Kirsch Praline Delights

125 g (4 ½ oz) unsalted butter, softened
300 g (10 ½ oz) dark (plain or semi-sweet) chocolate, melted
60 ml (2 fl oz) Kirsch liqueur
cocoa powder, sifted, for rolling

Place the softened butter into a mixing bowl and cream until almost white and very light. Add the melted chocolate to the butter and then the Kirsch. Mix until all ingredients are combined into a smooth paste. When mixed, place the mixture into a piping (pastry) bag fitted with a 1 cm (⅓ in) plain round nozzle. Pipe small straight shapes on to a baking tray (sheet) lined with baking parchment. These shapes should be approximately 3 cm (1 in) long.

When all the mixture has been piped, place the tray in the refrigerator for 2 hours to allow the pralines to set hard. Remove and roll each praline lightly in the sifted cocoa powder. Refrigerate until ready to serve.

Makes 30–36

1. Cream the butter until almost white, add the melted chocolate and then the Kirsch.

2. Pipe 3 cm (1 in) shapes of the mixture on to a baking tray lined with baking parchment.

3. When set firm roll lightly in sifted cocoa powder.

Triple Chocolate Spice Cookies (above), Baked Chocolate Tuiles (below)

CHAPTER TWO

Cooking with Chocolate

Some 500 years after its introduction to Europe, the range of chocolate available has grown. The cook and connoisseur can now choose from white, dark (plain or semi-sweet) or milk chocolate.

◆

All these kinds of chocolates can be combined with other ingredients and baked into the most sinfully delicious desserts ever imagined. Cakes, cookies, slices and muffins are more popular when they include even a little chocolate (but the more the better!).

Baked Chocolate Tuiles

◆

If the tuiles become cold and firm before you have finished shaping them, reheat them on a baking tray (sheet) in the oven for 1–2 minutes or until they become soft and malleable.

6 egg whites
1 cup (7 oz) icing (powdered) sugar, sifted
½ cup (2 oz) plain (all-purpose) flour, sifted
1 tablespoon cocoa powder, sifted
75 g (2 ½ oz) unsalted butter, melted

Preheat oven to 180°C (350°F) and lightly grease a baking tray (sheet).

Mix the egg whites with the sifted icing sugar until incorporated. Add the flour and cocoa and lightly whisk until a smooth paste is formed. Allow the batter to rest for 15 minutes.

Stir in the melted butter and mix well. Place tablespoons of the batter on to the prepared tray and spread into 5–8 cm (2–3 in) circles.

Bake for 10 minutes in the pre-heated oven. Remove the tuiles from the tray by sliding a flat knife underneath each one. Press each tuile immediately around a rolling pin or cylindrical object so that it hardens into a semi-circular shape.

Makes 18–24

Triple Chocolate Spice Cookies

180 g (6 oz) unsalted butter, softened
1 cup (6 oz) soft (light) brown sugar
¼ cup (3 oz) golden (dark corn) syrup
1 egg
2 cups (8 ½ oz) plain (all-purpose) flour
2 teaspoons baking powder
2 tablespoons cocoa powder
2 teaspoons cinnamon
30 g (1 oz) white chocolate, finely chopped
30 g (1 oz) milk chocolate, finely chopped
white, milk and dark (plain or semi-sweet) chocolate, melted, for drizzling

Place the butter, sugar and golden syrup in a mixing bowl and cream until light and fluffy. Add the egg and mix until combined. Sift all the dry ingredients together and add one half of the dry ingredients at a time to the creamed mixture. Mix well. Fold in the finely chopped white and milk chocolate. Cover with plastic (cling) wrap and refrigerator for 45 minutes.

Preheat oven to 180°C (350°F). Line a baking tray (sheet) with baking parchment.

Remove the mixture from the refrigerator. Take walnut-sized portions, roll them into balls and place on the prepared tray. Allow at least 5 cm (2 in) between each cookie for spreading. Bake in the preheated oven 12–15 minutes. Remove from the oven and allow to cool slightly on the tray before placing on a wire cooling rack. Once the cookies are cool, drizzle them with a small amount of melted white, milk and dark (plain or semi-sweet) chocolate.

Makes 24

Sacher Torte

---

1 ¼ cups (5 oz) plain (all-purpose) flour
¼ cup (1 ½ oz) cocoa powder
180 g (6 oz) unsalted butter
⅓ cup (3 ½ oz) caster (superfine) sugar
7 eggs, separated into yolks and whites
¼ cup (1 ½ oz) ground almonds
1 cup (10 ½ oz) ground hazelnuts
⅔ cup (5 ½ oz) caster (superfine) sugar
1 cup (10 ½ oz) apricot jam
300 g (10 ½ oz) marzipan (see p. 62)
360 g (12 ½ oz) dark (plain or semi-sweet) chocolate, melted
60 g (2 oz) milk chocolate, melted

Preheat oven to 180°C (350°F). Grease a 23 cm (9 in) springform pan lightly with butter and line it with baking parchment.

Mix the flour and cocoa together and sift twice. Beat the butter and the first amount of sugar in a separate bowl until creamy, light and fluffy. Gradually add the egg yolks and beat well. Gently fold in by hand the flour, cocoa, almonds and hazelnuts. Beat the egg whites separately until stiff peaks form. Gradually add the second amount of the sugar to the egg whites a spoonful at a time. Beat until the sugar has dissolved. Take a quarter of the beaten egg whites and gently mix into the stiff chocolate mixture by hand. Very carefully fold in the remaining egg whites. Pour the mixture into the prepared pan and bake in the preheated oven 35–40 minutes or until the top of the cake is firm to touch.

Cool in the pan for 5 minutes before turning out on to a wire cooling rack. When cold cut into quarters horizontally. Spread each layer thinly with apricot then stack one on top of the other. Spread the remaining apricot jam over the top and sides of the cake. On a lightly floured surface, roll the marzipan thinly enough so that it will cover the top and sides of the jam-covered cake. Cover the cake with marzipan. Spread the melted dark chocolate over the top and sides of the cake using a warm palette knife. Make sure that the chocolate is completely smooth and free of air bubbles. As the chocolate begins to set, use a large hot knife to mark the chocolate into 12 segments from which it will be cut later. When the chocolate coating has begun to set, use a small paper piping (pastry) bag (see p. 55) of melted milk chocolate to pipe the word 'Sacher' on each portion of the cake. Place cake in the refrigerator until ready to serve.

Serves 12

Sacher Torte

Chocolate Pear Shortcake

Chocolate Pear Shortcake

◆

300 g (10 ½ oz) unsalted butter
1 ½ cups (10 ½ oz) caster
(superfine) sugar
3 eggs
2 ¼ cups (9 ½ oz) plain
(all-purpose) flour
2 tablespoons cocoa powder
1 teaspoon ground cinnamon
1 teaspoon mixed spice (see note below)
1 teaspoon baking powder
300 g (10 ½ oz) tinned pears, sliced
icing (powdered) sugar, for dusting

Preheat oven to 180°C (350°F).
Lightly grease and line a 23 cm (9 in)
springform cake pan with baking
parchment.

Cream the butter and sugar
together until light and fluffy. Add
the eggs one at a time and continue
mixing until well combined. Sift the
flour, cocoa, spices and baking powder into the creamed butter and egg
mixture. Continue mixing until well
incorporated. Spread half of the mixture evenly over the base of the pan.
Arrange the sliced pears on top then
carefully cover the pears with
the remaining cake mixture. Bake in
the preheated oven 45–55 minutes.
Cool in the pan. Dust with icing
sugar and cut into wedges.
Note: If you cannot buy mixed spice
you can make it by combining ½
teaspoon ground cinnamon, ¼
teaspoon ground ginger, a pinch of
ground nutmeg and a pinch of
ground cloves.

Serves 12

Chocolate Coconut Slice

◆

180 g (6 oz) unsalted butter
2 ¼ cups (12 ½ oz) soft (light) brown
sugar
1 ¾ cups (7 ½ oz) plain
(all-purpose) flour
2 tablespoons (2 oz) raspberry jam
3 eggs
1 teaspoon baking powder, sifted
1 tablespoon cocoa powder
1 cup (3 oz) desiccated (shredded)
coconut
1 ¼ cups (5 oz) walnuts, chopped
icing (powdered) sugar,
for dusting

Preheat oven to 180°C (350°F).
Grease and line an 18 x 28 x 2 cm
(7 x 11 x ¾ in) baking tray (sheet).

Cream the butter and ¾ cup (4 oz)
only of the brown sugar until light
and pale in colour. Add 1 ½ cups
(6 oz) only of the flour and mix to a
crumbly texture. Press the mixture
into the prepared tray and bake in
preheated oven 25 minutes or until
golden brown. Remove from oven and
allow to cool. Maintain oven temperature. When the base is cool, spread
it thinly with raspberry jam. Beat the
eggs until they are light and fluffy.
Add the remaining brown sugar and
flour and the baking powder and
cocoa. Stir in the coconut and walnuts. Spread mixture over the jam-
covered base and bake for a further
30–35 minutes. Cut into portions
while still warm, dust with icing
sugar. Allow to cool before serving.

Makes 20–24

Chocolate Coconut Slice

Chocolate Macaroon Sticks

Chocolate Macaroon Sticks

◆

2 egg whites
½ cup (4 oz) caster (superfine) sugar
2 tablespoons (½ oz) hot chocolate
drinking powder
1 ½ cups (5 oz) desiccated
(shredded) coconut
2 tablespoons (½ oz) cocoa, sifted
½ cup (3 oz) icing (powdered) sugar
2 tablespoons hot water
extra icing (powdered) sugar,
for dusting

Preheat oven to 160°C (320°F).
Lightly grease two baking trays
(sheets).

Whisk the egg whites until stiff
peaks form. Mix the caster sugar with
the chocolate drinking powder and
very slowly add to the egg whites.
Beat until stiff. Stir in the coconut.
Using a piping (pastry) bag fitted with
a 1 cm (⅓ in) plain round nozzle, pipe
the mixture into 5 cm (2 in) lengths
on to the prepared trays. Bake in the
preheated oven 35–40 minutes. Cool
on the trays.

Mix the sifted cocoa, icing sugar
and hot water in a saucepan and
warm for a few seconds over a low
heat. Dip one end of the baked macaroon sticks into the icing, then place
on to a sheet of baking parchment to
dry. Dust the other end with icing
sugar before serving.

Makes 15–18

Chocolate Chip and Banana Muffins

3 ¼ cups (14 oz) plain
(all-purpose) flour
1 tablespoon baking powder
¾ cup (4 oz) soft (light) brown sugar
½ cup (4 oz) caster (superfine) sugar
½ cup (4 oz) chocolate chips (drops)
2 ½ cups (4 oz) shredded (flaked)
coconut
2 large ripe bananas, lightly mashed
300 ml (10 fl oz) milk
120 g (4 oz) butter, melted
2 eggs, lightly beaten
3 tablespoons caster (superfine) sugar
1 teaspoon ground cinnamon

Preheat oven to 180°C (350°F).
Lightly grease a patty (muffin) pan.
Sift the flour and baking powder.
Add the brown sugar, caster sugar,
chocolate chips, coconut and lightly
mashed bananas. Add the milk,
melted butter and eggs and mix
through the dry ingredients until all
are combined. Fill three quarters of
each muffin mould with the mixture.
Mix the extra caster sugar with the
cinnamon and sprinkle this on top of
each muffin. Bake in the preheated
oven 20 minutes. When baked, cool
in the tray for 5 minutes, then
remove each muffin carefully from
the pan and cool on a wire cooling
rack.

Makes 15

Chocolate Chip and Banana Muffins

Spicy Fingers

Spicy Fingers

◆

390 g (14 oz) unsalted butter
1 cup (12 ½ oz) golden
(dark corn) syrup
1 egg
1 cup (6 oz) soft (light) brown sugar
3 ¼ cups (14 oz) plain (all-purpose)
flour
1 ½ teaspoons bicarbonate of soda
(baking soda)
1 ½ teaspoons ground ginger
1 ½ teaspoons ground cinnamon
125 ml (4 ½ fl oz) boiling water
2 tablespoons sour (soured) cream
210 g (7 ½ oz) chocolate chips (drops)
or dark (plain or semi-sweet) chocolate,
finely chopped
icing (powdered) sugar,
for dusting

Preheat oven to 180°C (350°F).
Grease and line a 25 x 30 x 3 cm
(10 x 11 x 1 in) baking tray (sheet)
with baking parchment.

Place the butter and syrup into
a saucepan and heat slowly until
melted. Add the egg and sugar, stirring continuously. Sift the flour,
bicarbonate of soda and the spices
together into a bowl. Add the egg
mixture and water to the dry ingredients and mix quickly until smooth.
Add the sour cream and the chocolate
chips and stir through. Spread the
mixture on to the prepared tray and
bake in the preheated oven 25–35
minutes or until a skewer inserted
into the centre comes out clean. Cool
in the tray and dust with icing sugar
before cutting into fingers.

Makes 24

Orange Streusel Muffins

3 cups (12 ½ oz) plain (all-purpose)
flour
3 tablespoons cocoa powder
1 tablespoon baking powder
1 ½ cups (8 ½ oz) soft (light) brown
sugar
100 g (3 ½ oz) chocolate chips (drops)
or dark (plain or semi-sweet) chocolate,
finely chopped
zest and juice of 1 large orange
300 ml (10 ½ fl oz) milk
120 g (4 oz) unsalted butter, melted
2 eggs

STREUSEL
½ cup (2 oz) plain (all-purpose) flour
1 teaspoon ground cinnamon
¼ cup (1 oz) ground almonds
¼ cup (1 oz) caster (superfine) sugar
60 g (2 oz) unsalted butter
icing (powdered) sugar, for dusting

Preheat oven to 160°C (320°F).
Grease well a patty (muffin) pan.

Sift the flour, cocoa powder and
baking powder. Stir in the brown
sugar and chocolate chips. Mix the
orange juice and zest, milk, melted
butter and eggs through the dry
ingredients until all are combined.
Fill each of the muffin moulds up to
three quarters. Sprinkle a little of the
streusel on to each muffin and bake
in the preheated oven 20–25 minutes. When baked allow the muffins
to cool in the pan for 10 minutes
before carefully removing them. Cool
on a wire cooling rack and dust with
icing sugar.

STREUSEL
Place the flour, cinnamon, almonds
and sugar into a mixing bowl and add
the butter. Crumb the butter through
the dry ingredients until the mixture
resembles fresh breadcrumbs.

Makes 15

Orange Streusel Muffins

Fondue

Fondue

½ cup (5 oz) liquid glucose (corn) syrup
150 ml (5 fl oz) thickened (double
or heavy) cream
30 ml (1 fl oz) Grand Marnier liqueur
or your favourite liqueur
240 g (8 ½ oz) dark (plain or
semi-sweet) chocolate, chopped
selection of fresh fruits (perhaps
strawberries, grapes, pineapple,
mandarin or orange segments),
marinated for 1 hour in 30 ml
(1 fl oz) Grand Marnier liqueur
or your favourite liqueur

Gently heat the glucose, thickened cream and your choice of liqueur in a saucepan and stir until boiled. Remove the saucepan from the heat, add the chopped chocolate and stir until all the ingredients are combined. Serve immediately with a selection of marinated fresh fruits.
Note: You can substitute the dark (plain or semi-sweet) chocolate with white or milk chocolate in this recipe. You can also make one mixture from all three types of chocolate by pouring them into one dish and allowing them to become a marbled mass.

Serves 6–8

Supreme Mousse

6 egg yolks
1 cup (7 ½ oz) icing (powdered) sugar
240 g (8 ½ oz) unsalted butter,
softened
¼ cup (1 oz) cocoa powder
150 g (5 oz) dark (plain or semi-sweet)
chocolate, melted
300 ml (10 ½ fl oz) thickened (double
or heavy) cream

Place the egg yolks and ½ cup (3 ½ oz) only of the icing sugar into the bowl and whisk until thick, light and fluffy. In a separate bowl, cream together the butter and cocoa until light and fluffy. Whisk the melted chocolate into the egg yolk mixture, then fold through the butter mixture and combine all ingredients thoroughly.

Place the cream and the remaining icing sugar into a bowl and whisk to a soft peak, before folding through the chocolate mixture. Pour the Supreme Mousse into fluted glasses or chocolate cups and chill for 2 hours before serving.

Note: This mousse can be served inside the decorative chocolate collars (see p. 54).

Makes 6–8 dessert portions

Supreme Mousse

Basic equipment needed for decorating with chocolate

CHAPTER THREE

Decorating with Chocolate

Whether you use it in shavings, curls or squares, the unique taste of chocolate finishes off any dessert or petit four. Decorating with chocolate is surprisingly simple. All it takes is a little practice and a love of that magic ingredient — chocolate!

◆

If you are ever feeling guilty about eating chocolate, don't forget that it is rich in carbohydrates and is an excellent source of energy in a concentrated form. That is why it is always included in emergency rations.

WHICH CHOCOLATE TO USE?

Two varieties of chocolate can be used in this book: couverture chocolate and compound chocolate.

Couverture (pure cooking) chocolate is a pure form of chocolate which contains cocoa butter. If required for setting or moulding it needs to be prepared using a complicated and specialised process called tempering. For this reason, couverture chocolate is only used for its superior flavour and palatability and not for decoration.

Compound chocolate is more readily available and is made using vegetable fats instead of cocoa butter. This chocolate requires no special techniques and is used for all chocolate recipes but especially for coating cakes, making chocolate curls and collars and for piping.

Melting Chocolate

◆

The easiest way to melt chocolate is in a double boiler or in a bowl over a pot of simmering water. Break the chocolate into small pieces to speed up the melting process. Place a saucepan of water over the heat and allow the water to simmer. Remove the saucepan from the heat and place the chocolate into a glass or stainless steel bowl which is just large enough to rest over the saucepan. Place the bowl over the hot water. Never allow the chocolate to come into contact with the water and stir the chocolate until it liquefies. Keep the chocolate liquefied while working on other parts of your recipe. You may need to place the bowl over simmering water in cold weather.

Melting or melted chocolate should never be covered as condensed water on the lid can fall back into the chocolate. Even a small amount of water in the melted chocolate will make it thicken and turn into a solid mass.

To cover a cake with chocolate, follow the method given in the particular recipe, but always remember to work quickly and spread the chocolate thinly. To cover one 23 cm (9 in) cake use 400 g (14 oz) of melted chocolate; however, if the cake is simply to be brushed over with chocolate using a pastry brush, 300 g (10 ½ oz) will be sufficient.

Making Decorative Collars

◆

Chocolate collars add a special and decorative finish to any cake. Measure the height of the cake to be decorated and cut a strip of baking parchment 1 cm (⅓ in) higher than the depth of the cake. This strip should also be long enough to wrap easily around the circumference of the cake with 1 cm to spare.

1. Spread the chocolate thinly and evenly over the strip of baking parchment.

2. Carefully wrap the chocolate coated strip around the outside of the cake.

For a 25 cm (10 in) strip of baking parchment to wrap around a 23 cm (9 in) cake, spread 300 g (10 ½ oz) of melted dark (plain or semi-sweet) chocolate over the parchment and spread thinly and evenly. As soon as the parchment is covered, very carefully pick it up lengthways and wrap it around the cake, parchment face out. You can cut off any excess if it is too long for the cake. Smooth the paper around the cake and chill in the refrigerator for 5–10 minutes or until the collar has set firm. Peel the parchment from the chocolate.

Note: Supreme Chocolate Mousse (see p. 50) can be served inside chocolate collars by simply piping the mousse into the centre of the collar.

Piping

Before piping directly on to any finished pastry item, practise on a piece of baking parchment.

To pipe, spoon a small amount of melted chocolate into a small paper piping (pastry) bag. Make sure no lumps of chocolate are present. Fold over the ends of the bag. Cut the tip of the bag to the desired size. Practise designs on parchment and allow the chocolate to set. If desired, these designs, once set, can then be carefully peeled from the paper and placed on top of a cake.

To make unusual decorative designs for special occasions, draw an outline of the figure required and place a sheet of baking parchment over the top.

Using a thin-tipped paper piping (pastry) bag filled with chocolate, trace the drawn design on the top sheet. Allow this outline to set firm. Then use the thin-tipped paper piping (pastry) bag filled with another colour chocolate, to fill in all the gaps inside the design. Take extra care you do not go over the top of the outline of the design. Once you have completed filling the gaps, allow to set till firm, then peel from the paper.

Decorative Shavings

◆

*Approximately 250 g (9 oz) of milk,
dark (plain or semi-sweet) or white
chocolate will make enough shavings
to cover a 23 cm (9 in) cake.*

Pull a vegetable peeler smoothly and
evenly across the surface of a block of
chocolate. This will produce small
shavings which are great for spreading
on cakes or for rolling truffles.

Decorative Curls

◆

*Approximately 500 g (17 ½ oz) each
of dark (plain or semi-sweet) chocolate
will make enough curls to cover a
23 cm (9 in) cake.*

Pour melted dark (plain or semi-
sweet) chocolate on to a marble slab
or a stainless steel bench (counter)
top and use a palette knife to spread
thinly. As the chocolate begins to set,
hold a large knife at a 45° angle to

the bench or surface and pull gently
through the chocolate. It is essential
to work quickly or the chocolate will
harden and splinter.

Two-Tone Curls

◆

*Approximately 250 g (9 oz) combined
weight of white chocolate and dark
(plain or semi-sweet) chocolate will
make enough curls to cover a
23 cm (9 in) cake.*

Pour melted white chocolate on to a
marble slab or stainless steel bench
(counter) top and use a palette knife
to spread thinly. Make ridges in one

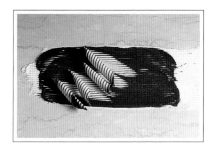

direction with a comb scraper or fork. Allow to cool and harden. Pour melted dark chocolate over the top of the ridges of white chocolate. Spread thinly until the white chocolate is completely covered. As the chocolate begins to set, pull a large knife with a flexible blade at a 45° angle to the bench (counter) top through the chocolate.

Triple Curls

---◆---

Approximately 210 g (7 ½ oz) each of white, milk and dark (plain or semi-sweet) chocolate will make enough curls to cover a 23 cm (9 in) cake.

Melt each kind of chocolate separately and pour each into a separate paper piping (pastry) bag. Pipe rows of dark chocolate on to a marble slab or stainless steel bench (counter) top. Leave enough room between each row of dark chocolate to pipe the other two chocolates. Working quickly, pipe in the rows of milk and then white

chocolate making certain that each chocolate is touching the other as it sets. Allow the chocolate to firm slightly before pulling a large knife with a flexible blade at a 45° angle to the bench (counter) top through the chocolate to produce the curls.

Marbled Curls

---◆---

Approximately 100 g (3 ½ oz) each of white, milk and dark (plain or semi-sweet) chocolate will make enough marbled curls to cover a 23 cm (9 in) cake.

Drizzle melted white chocolate in a very abstract fashion on to a marble slab or stainless steel bench (counter) top. Over the top of the white chocolate drizzle the milk chocolate in a different pattern. Allow the white and milk chocolate to set together. Pour dark (plain or semi-sweet) chocolate over the top of the white and milk chocolate to create the finished marble effect. Spread it thinly.

Allow it to set but not completely harden before pulling a large knife with a flexible blade at a 45° angle to the bench (counter) top through the chocolate to produce curls.

Decorative Squares

◆

Approximately 400 g (14 oz) of melted dark (plain or semi-sweet) chocolate will make 20–30 chocolate squares.

Use a palette knife to spread the chocolate evenly on to a sheet of baking parchment 30 x 30 cm (12 x 12 in). Leave in a cool place to set for 5–10 minutes. Mark 5 x 5 cm (2 x 2 in) squares on to the chocolate and using a clean sharp knife cut the chocolate where it has been marked. If the chocolate has set too hard and is shattering at the slightest touch, use a hot sharp knife for cutting. **Note:** Chocolate squares can be used to decorate the top or sides of any cake.

Modelling Chocolate

◆

Approximately 225 g (8 oz) of liquid glucose (corn) syrup and 300 g (10 ½ oz) of melted dark (plain or semi-sweet) chocolate will cover a 23 cm (9 in) cake.

Place the syrup in a saucepan and heat until it liquefies. Remove from the heat and mix in the chocolate. Continue to stir until the mixture leaves the sides of the pan. Pour into a container lined with plastic (cling) wrap and allow to set at room temperature. Do not chill.

When the chocolate has set, roll out on to a lightly floured surface until it is very thin (approximately 3–4 mm in thickness) and fits the cake to be decorated. Stretch the chocolate in your hands so it is about one and a half times the surface area of the cake. Holding the piece of chocolate in the centre, allow it to fall over the cake so that it looks ruffled.

Smooth down the sides of the chocolate against the cake. If the chocolate tears, tuck the torn area under and drape another piece of chocolate over the torn area.

Alternatively the cake can be covered smoothly by simply placing the chocolate layer on top of the cake, smoothing over and cutting away any excess chocolate from around the sides of the cake.

When the cake is completely covered with the modelling chocolate, dust lightly with cocoa powder. Modelling chocolate will store in a cool dry place for up to 6 months. Ensure it is not subject to dramatic changes in temperatures.

To Make a Centrepiece

◆

Whether crowning a cake or sitting by itself on a dessert buffet, there is nothing quite so dramatic as a beautifully produced chocolate centrepiece. Serve it by itself with coffee and simply allow your guests to sample the fine threads and lattices of chocolate in front of them. Take care and take your time with all centrepiece productions.

The following designs are meant as a guide only. There are an endless number of designs you can experiment with to create the most fantastic chocolate centrepieces.

Approximately 360 g (12 ½ oz) of melted dark (plain or semi-sweet) chocolate is needed for a centrepiece crown of a 23 cm (9 in) cake.

Cut four strips of baking parchment which are large enough to cover the shape of your centrepiece. Using the designs on page 60, place one sheet of baking parchment over one of the designs. Pipe the design with the chocolate using a paper piping (pastry) bag. This piping (pastry) bag (see p. 55) should be cut so that it has a thick nozzle. Pipe one of these designs four times and allow them to set in the refrigerator on a tray. Once set, take two of the designs and place them flat on a tray touching each other (one will have to be turned upside down so that they are facing each other). Join them using a small amount of melted chocolate on the two points that are touching, and allow this to set.

When this has set, pipe a small dot of chocolate on the previous joins and sit another of the piped pieces vertically on to this. Using your fingertips hold the centrepiece together until it has set firm and does not need to be held up.

Once firm, stand the centrepiece up so that it is resting on the base of all three joined pieces. Carefully pick up the fourth piece and with a little melted chocolate piped on to the same points, join it to the other three pieces. Allow this to set hard before placing on top of a cake.

Note: When making a centrepiece for the first time make 2–3 more designs than the four required to allow for breakages and so you can choose the best piped designs. If you need to store a centrepiece for a considerable time, strengthen the piped designs by turning each one over, once it is set, and piping the design over the top. By piping over the flat side (which was attached to the paper) you will enhance the appearance of the centrepiece. Allow the second side to set firm before joining the centrepiece as described.

1. Trace the design with chocolate on to baking parchment.

2. Firstly join two of the hardened chocolate designs together with melted chocolate. Once firm join the third piece vertically with melted chocolate. When this has hardened, stand it upright and with more melted chocolate join the fourth piece.

You will need to enlarge these designs to 14 ½ cm (5 ¾ in) high on a photocopier (Xerox machine) to get the actual size of the templates.

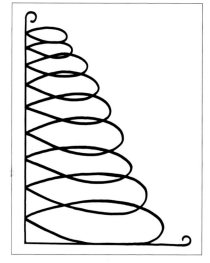

Centrepiece

Important Notes

◆

All ingredients should be at room temperature when used unless the recipe advises otherwise. Ensure that all utensils are clean, dry and grease free before cooking. Water or grease on utensils can adversely affect recipes, especially when using egg whites, which will not reach maximum aeration if mixed with even small amounts of grease or water.

EGG WEIGHTS

All eggs used in these recipes should be 55-60 g (approximately 2 oz).

BAKING TRAY (SHEET) SIZES

In all the recipes we have endeavoured to provide you with international tray sizes but if you find that the tray size suggested is not available please use the closest size you can find. For this reason you may need two trays when we suggest one.

MARZIPAN

Marzipan is a sweetened mixture of ground almonds, liquid glucose (corn) syrup and icing (powdered) sugar. It is also known as almond paste. Marzipan is available in a variety of sizes and packagings.

Marzipan can absorb moisture or dry out so careful storage is essential. If it absorbs moisture it will begin to dissolve. If marzipan dries out it will begin to ferment. To store marzipan, wrap it in plastic (cling) wrap and place it in an airtight container. Store at room temperature in a dark place for up to three weeks.

To bake marzipan it must have a higher proportion of almonds than sugar. If the proportion of sugar is too high, the marzipan will boil instead of bake, which will adversely affect the taste and appearance of the finished creation. The preferred ratio of marzipan is 66 % almond and 34% sugar.

OVEN TEMPERATURES AND GAS MARKS

DEGREES (F)	200	225	250	275	300	325	350	375	400	425	450
GAS MARK 1	¼	½	1	2	3	4	5	6	7	8	9
GAS MARK 2	1	2	3	4	5	6	7	8	9	10	11

Acknowledgements

The author would like to thank the following people and organisations for their assistance and support:

Gwen Gedeon, from The Welsh Lady Patisserie, for her professional generosity

Brian Cox, General Manager, Socomin International Fine Foods,
for their Odense range of products

Paul Frizzel, Account Executive, Sunny Queen Eggs

Anna Permezel, James Tan, Rod Slater and Kay Cafarella of Cadbury Confectionery

Juliet Van Den Heuval, the Prestige Group

J.D. Millner and Associates, for their Le Creuset range of products

Jan Liddle, Glad Products of Australia

The promotions team at Myer Brisbane City Store

Sally Armonoras, Queensco United Dairy Foods

John Reid, Defiance Milling

John Dart, Trumps Nuts and Dried Fruits

Ian Elliot, CSR, for their range of sugar products

Lois Stocks, author of The Home Confectioner

Designer Trim Pty Ltd, Surry Hills, NSW & Richmond, Vic

Index